VALUES

(Three one act plays)

The Spraying of John O'Dorey
Backwater
The Pure of Heart

Other books by the author

Values

(Three one act plays)

by

JOHN B. KEANE

Foreword by
FLOR DULLEA

THE MERCIER PRESS
DUBLIN AND CORK

THE MERCIER PRESS
4 Bridge Street, Cork
25 Lower Abbey Street, Dublin 1

© John B. Keane, 1973

SBN 85342 369 5

These plays had their premiere by the Theatre of the South, in Cork on 25 April, 1973.

The cast were

THE SPRAYING OF JOHN O'DOREY

The Judge	Mary O'Donovan
Mr. Crystal, B.L.	Michael Twomey
Mr. Fog, B.L.	Donal O'Sullivan
Court Clerk	Dick Healy
John O'Dorey	Eamon Nash
Professor Hubert Analis	Flor Dullea
Miss Lily Malone, S.P.G.C.	Mary Foley
Mary O'Dorey	Norma Gleeson

BACKWATER

Jimmy	Eamon Nash
Sammy	Donal O'Sullivan
Eddie	Flor Dullea
Mrs. Swan	Mary O'Donovan

THE PURE OF HEART

Murt O'Brien	Eamon Nash
Bartholomew Lane	Michael Twomey
Alaphonsus Fonce, a tramp	James N. Healy

Decor by Bill Coughlan
Produced by Dan Donovan and Flor Dullea

TO

PHIL KEANE

CONTENTS

FOREWORD

J. B. Keane is Ireland's most prolific dramatist, a volcano who increasingly pours out theatrical-lava scorching with dramatic invention. In the fifteen years since SIVE gave a new dimension to native Irish writing, his imagination has been ceaselessly looking for fresh modes of expression. That he has allowed it to run its course is the punters good luck. He constantly parades a winner. John B's latest invention, entitled VALUES has indelibly stamped on it the label of success.

On 25 April 1973 at the Group Theatre, Cork, the Theatre of the South premiered VALUES. As on so many previous occasions when Keane's work was premiered in Cork, the theatre was packed with an expectant audience. On this occasion John B. has broken new ground with three thematically connected one-act plays, and all wondered what new delights awaited them. They were not disappointed for VALUES took a look at some facets of Irish life and sifted them with ingenious insight.

The first offering THE SPRAYING OF JOHN O'DOREY took a futuristic look at pollution. Set in a courtroom, and played in a stylistic manner, we were led to laugh at the inanities to which ultra-conservationists may be led by the year 2052 in preserving the environment. The killing of the avaricious flea could be acclaimed as a murderous act. The breaking of the commandment of conservation is punishable by death, a death painlessly performed due to the invention of new type, lethal weapons. John B. smiles at the idea that people may perhaps be more expendable than the environmental creatures.

The second play BACKWATER is a realistic drama, which gives value to lonliness, indifference and the ingratitude of an only son to his widowed mother. The tear and the smile are at each others heels. This is vintage Keane where the simplest commonplace talk

9

has the audience in uproars. Then there are the hand-kerchief moments in scenes between the mother and her insensitive son and again between the mother and her new found friend. In BACKWATER John B. has written a one-act play which can stand any test of dramatic writing. It ranks with the best short plays of Synge, T. C. Murray and Eugene O'Neill.

THE PURE OF HEART is a hilarious situation farce which takes as its value the moral hypocrisy which places adultery far higher up the ladder of iniquity than cold-blooded murder. John B. looks at the fifth and sixth commandments and highlights their importance in the hierarchy of religious interpretation. In doing so he has created a memorable piece of theatre, using a simple roadside setting, a June night and three characters as varied in their attitudes to life and love as one could possibly imagine. For them he has written dialogue that sparkles as a glow-worm on a June night. As in the other plays, here again there is perfect form in the writing, a unity of place and time, a quick intro-duction of the characters, no superfluous dialogue and surprise endings reminiscent of Maupassant and O. Henry at their best.

Flor Dullea, Cork 1974.

THE SPRAYING OF JOHN O'DOREY

A play in one act

CHARACTERS IN ORDER OF APPEARANCE:

JUDGE.

CLERK.

MR. CRYSTAL.

MR. FOG.

POLICEMAN.

JOHN O'DOREY.

PROFESSOR HUBERT ANALIS.

MISS LILY MALONE.

MARY O'DOREY.

Action takes place in a courtroom sometime in the future. On the bench sits a female judge. At the side sits the Court Clerk. There is an empty dock. There are a number of witnesses male and female. There are the counsels for prosecution and defence. There is a hum of conversation as the curtain rises. Having inspected some papers the judge raps for order with her gavel. There is immediate silence.

JUDGE What's next?

CLERK (*Rises*) My lord the next case is John O'Dorey versus the State.

JUDGE Call John O'Dorey.

CLERK Call John O'Dorey.

JUDGE The prosecution may proceed and for God's sake

11

Mr. Crystal be as concise as possible. We don't want
to spend all day.

(*Stands and dons his spectacles. He takes a sheaf of
papers from the desk*).

(*Enter John O'Dorey followed by a uniformed policeman
who escorts him to the bench*).

POLICEMAN Here stands the accused John O'Dorey my
lord.

JUDGE (*To policeman*) You're excused.

(*Policeman bows his head and brings the palms of his
hands together. He slowly backs out of courtroom*).

JUDGE You answer to the name of John O'Dorey?

JOHN Yes my lord.

JUDGE And you are indeed the John O'Dorey summoned
here on a capital charge this day.

JOHN Yes my lord.

JUDGE Go to the dock and stay there.

JOHN Yes my lord.

JUDGE Please proceed Mister Crystal.

MR. C. My lord the prosecution will show that the same
John O'Dorey as now occupies that very dock before
our eyes is guilty of the wanton murder of one pink
earthworm, one brace of adult titmice, one cock
sparrow, eleven beatles, nine humming bees, twenty
four assorted bugs catalogued by Professor Moses
Moran not in court, one brooding wagtail, one whole
school of one hundred and twenty seven infant
minnows, three hen salmon fry and one fully grown
green-breasted grenadine butterfly believed to be the
last of its species. There is also a Jenny wren in a
critical condition and a white moth not expected to
live. The prosecution will show that the aforesaid
Johnny O'Dorey (*Takes off his spectacles and looks
hard at O'Dorey. Replaces spectacles and proceeds*)
will show to the satisfaction of his lordship and the
entire court that the aforementioned O'Dorey did empty
a two gallon enamel bucket of sour goats milk into
a stream near his home thereby causing the death and

12

ailments of the creatures cited by me on this day of
our Lord, the first of October two thousand and
fifty two.

JUDGE (*To John*) How say you sir?

JOHN Not guilty my lord.

(*Judge makes notes while Court Clerk rises and hands
Bible to John*).

CLERK Do you solemnly swear to tell the truth the whole
truth and nothing but the truth so help you God . . .
Say I do.

JOHN I do.

(*Clerk returns to his seat.*)

MR. C. (*To John*) It's not your first time in court.

JOHN That is correct.

MR. C. In fact you have been here a number of times.

JOHN That is correct.

MR. C. You have also been in jail a number of times.

JOHN That is correct.

(*Another counsel rises. He is Mr. Fog for the defence.*)

MR. F. I object.

JUDGE What grounds?

MR. F. On the grounds that his former convictions have
no bearing on this present case.

MR. C. My lord I am trying to show the court that John
O'Dorey is an unmitigated scoundrel, a subhuman
wretch with a shady past and that it was inevitable
with a background like his that he would one day
face this court on a capital charge of this nature.

MR. F. Why not let the court decide whether he is subhuman or not?

JUDGE The court will decide in due course Mister Fog.
Pray proceed Mr. Crystal.

MR. C. (*To John*) Do you fart?

JOHN Eh?

MR. C. Do you fart? F . . . A . . . R . . . T.

JOHN Yes.

MR. C. Don't you know that farting was outlawed in the
year nineteen-eighty-eight by a special amendment to

the constitution, that provision was made under the Dangerous Explosives Act, subsection thirty one, for the apprehension and prosecution of all known farters.

JOHN Yes.

MR. C. Yet you persist in carrying on with this odious and illegal practice.

JOHN I have no control over it.

MR. C. There are pills.

JOHN They make me sick.

MR. C. That's no excuse. You received a two year jail sentence in 2039 for causing pollution. What sort of pollution?

JOHN I forget.

MR. C. Let me refresh your memory (*Reads from document.*) You John O'Dotey were convicted of farting severally in an enclosed place thereby causing temporary pollution of an area not less than ten thousand cubic feet. The place was MacMenamin's public house of Tubbergorm in the county of Kerry. You thereby created discomfort and distress for other convenient souls in that some were forced to vacate the area polluted by you. Do you deny it?

JOHN It's true.

MR. C. In twenty forty four you received a suspended sentence for sneezing in church. In twenty forty seven (*Finds info in documents*) you were convicted of spitting in a public place and sentenced to eighteen months with hard labour. In twenty forty nine you were convicted of deliberate dumping of date stones, orange peel and apple butts. For this you received a jail sentence of two years.

MR. F. My lord I must object. All this tedious biographical material cannot be considered as evidence.

MR. C. My lord I am attempting to define the exact character of the witness for the purpose of assessing his ultimate criminal possibilities and in doing this I feel I am doing a service to the court and indeed to all mankind.

14

JUDGE Objection overruled.

MR. C. I am endeavouring to confirm that if this perverted monster, this prosopopoiea of evil is permitted to live for another day human existence will be further jeopardised and our children will revert to the sickly shapes of the nineteen eighties and ninties when mankind was all but stunk out of existence.

(There is some applause and cheering to be heard from the body of the court.)

(Annoyed the Judge raps her gavel.)

JUDGE Any further emotional outbreaks and I will clear the court.

MR. C. With your kind permission my lord I will call the first witness.

JUDGE *(To John)* Step down.

(John steps down and sits near his counsel.)

MR. C. I call Professor Hubert Analis the state analyst.

JUDGE Call Professor Hubert Analis.

CLERK Call Professor Hubert Analis.

(Enter Professor Analis, a scholarly man of considerable years. He enters dock and is sworn.)

MR. C. You are Professor Hubert Analis.

PROF. Yes, I am he.

MR. C. On June seventh two thousand and fifty two you took certain objects from the stream known as the Awnygilly contiguous to the abode of the accused John O'Dorey.

PROF. That is so.

MR. C. Will you tell the court what those objects were?

PROF. Those objects my lord were an assortment of dead creatures which had been poisoned by bacteria.

MR. C. What sort of bacteria? In simple language so that the court will not be confused by scientific terminology.

PROF. A body of bacteria common to milk.

MR. C. What sort of milk?

PROF. Sour milk.

MR. C. Are you in a position to tell us exactly what sort

of sour milk caused the annihilation of these innocent creatures.

PROF. Sour goat's milk.

MR. C. Thank you professor. (*To Mr. Fog*) Your witness Mister Fog.

MR. F. I will not go into your qualifications Professor Analis. The court knows that they are in order and I might add knows that you are regarded as one of the most distinguished analysts in what we euphemistically call the civilised world. What age are you?

(*Professor Analis does not answer.*)

MR. F. I will repeat the question. What age are you?

(*An embarrassed Professor looks for help to the judge.*)

PROF. Must I answer?

JUDGE Unless you can provide adequate grounds why you should not.

PROF. My lord my wife died two years ago. Of late I have paid court to a girl of tender years. I have some hopes that she may not turn a deaf ear to a proposal of marriage. The only factor not in my favour is my age. I would assure his lordship that all my faculties are in first class working order due to my living a regular and athletic life. I believe that were I to disclose my age my chance of winning the hand of this most desirable maid would be greatly diminished. For this reason I would beg of the court to indulge me this once and I will openly and honestly answer all other questions that may be asked of me.

JUDGE Personally I have no desire to embarrass you Professor Analis but counsel for the defence has the right to expect an answer. How say you Mister Fog?

MR. F. I do not wish to embarrass the professor either. I will put the question another way and without rancour or ill-feeling wish the professor every success in his courtship. We must not interrupt the flow of true love.

(*There is some tittering from the body of the court. Judge raps gavel.*)

16

MR. F. Instead of telling me how old you are Professor would you tell me if you remember the days when home-made bread was a common item in the daily diet?

PROF. (*Glad to be off the hook*). Of course I do. My dear mother, God rest her, was a dab hand at dishing up the home made stuff. Potato cakes, soda cake, pointers of yellow meal bread and scones. Her scones were out of this world. As I recall she won a number of prizes at agricultural shows for brown bread. Her neighbours of course were most jealous. My mother was a paragon, an angel who thought of nought but her home and family.

MR. F. I hate to intrude on your little reverie Professor Analis but it's a shameful fact that the sordid business of the court must go on at the expense of those wonderful memories of your dear, departed mother. May we take it then from what you have just said that you yourself had a liking for your late mother's brown bread.

PROF. I couldn't get enough of it.

MR. F. How very touching. Perhaps you remember how this brown bread was made?

PROF. You may be sure I do.

MR. F. Would you tell the court?

PROF. Basically of course there was brown flour. This would be leavened with some soda and then there was margarine and of course sour milk. . . .

MR. F. (*Raises hand.*) Hold it Professor. Hold it right there. Did you say sour milk?

PROF. Yes.

MR. F. You are quite sure.

PROF. Yes.

MR. F. The same sour milk which you allege destroyed certain creatures in the Awnygilly stream.

PROF. Oh come now there s a vast amount of difference . . .

MR. F. The same sour milk which ended the career of the green-breasted grenadine butterfly and leaves ailing a small white moth and a sweet Jenny wren.

PROF. You are deliberately distorting. . . .

MR. F. The same sour milk which wipes out thousands of God's creatures but which in the case of Hubert Analis sends him, in the final stages of senility, rutting and rearing through the countryside after teenage girls when other old dotards of his age are saying their prayers and minding their grand-children . . .

(*Mr. Crystal jumps to his feet as does the Professor. There is general uproar. Judge raps with her gavel.*)

MR. C. I protest at this scurrilous attack on one of the country's most respected scientists. This is a black day for the legal profession when one of its members so debases himself.

MR. F. He is nothing but a manky old reprobate with women in the brain. He must be eighty if he's a day.

MR. C. The bar association will hear of this.

MR. F. I'm sure they'll enjoy it as much as I did.

(*The Judge raps at length with her gavel.*)

JUDGE I'm not altogether sure that you should not be admonished Mister Fog.

MR. F. I proved a point my lord. I believe that in this instance the end justified the means.

JUDGE You may step down Professor Analis.

PROF. Thank you my lord.

MR. C. I beg leave to call the next witness.

JUDGE Leave is granted.

MR. C. I call Miss Lily Malone of the S.P.G.C.

JUDGE Call Miss Lily Malone.

CLERK Call Miss Lily Malone.

(*Enter an oldish woman of dowdy appearance. She is alert and lively. She goes to dock and is sworn in.*)

MR. C. You are Miss Lily Malone.

LILY Yes.

MR. C. You are a member of the S.P.G.C.

LILY Yes.

MR. C. What do the letters S.P.G.C. stand for?

LILY Society for the Preservation of all God's Creatures.

MR. C. (*Repeats slowly, stressing each word.*) Society for the Preservation of all God's Creatures. (*To court.*) Not for the protection of themselves, nor you nor I, not for humans alone mark you but for each and every one of God's creatures. Miss Malone would you tell the court in your own words of the events which befell on the seventh day of June of this year.

LILY At eleven o'clock on June seventh I lay in hiding amid a cluster of hazel trees on the bank of the stream known as the Awnygilly.

MR. C. In hiding Miss Malone? Would you be good enough to elaborate?

LILY (*Scratches herself vigorously.*) There were reports of indiscriminate dumping into the Awnygilly stream and I was instructed by the secretary of the S.P.G.C. to take up a concealed position for as long as was necessary to identify the culprit and to charge him under the act.

MR. C. And pray did you succeed in your mission.

LILY Yes sir. At twelve o'clock on the dot a man appeared with a two gallon enamel bucket, the contents of which he dumped into the stream. I immediately rushed out from my hiding place and identified myself. I then charged him under the act and confiscated the bucket. (*Again she scratches herself vigorously.*)

MR. C. After you confiscated the bucket what happened?

LILY I examined the residue in the bucket and discovered it to be sour goat's milk.

MR. C. Is the man you charged on that occasion in this courtroom at this particular time

LILY He is.

MR. C. Would you point him out.

(*Lily points a finger at John O'Dorey.*)

LILY That is the man.

JUDGE Stand up sir.

(*John stands up.*)

JUDGE Are you sure beyond doubt that this is the man.

LILY I have no doubt whatsoever. (*Scratches herself vigorously.*)

MR. C. You have no doubt whatsoever that this . . . this creature John O'Dorey is the same person who emptied a two gallon enamel bucket of sour goat's milk into the stream known as the Awnygilly on the seventh day of June in this year of our Lord two thousand and fifty two.

LILY I have no doubt whatsoever.

MR. C. (*To Fog.*) Your witness.

MR. F. I submit that this witness is not reliable. I would ask that you instruct the clerk of the court that evidence given by her be erased from the records.

MR. C. This is preposterous.

JUDGE I will decide what is preposterous and what is not preposterous Mr. Crystal.

MR. C. Of course my lord. A slip of the tongue for which I am most contrite.

JUDGE Mr. Fog I must say that I am somewhat puzzled by your attitude towards Miss Malone. What you ask is impossible. There isn't a shred of evidence to show that she is unreliable.

MR. F. I will prove otherwise my lord. Miss Malone preaches preservation with one hand while with the other she harasses fleas and lice, pursues them relentlessly and kills for sheer pleasure. The monkey and the gorilla will kill fleas and lice for food but even they are not so sadistic as to kill for pleasure. She is a flea-killer my lord.

LILY I am not. I swear on my oath I am not.

MR. F. You are a flea-killer pure and simple and as such as arch a hypocrite as ever took an oath in this court-room.

MR. C. My lord I must protest in the most strenuous fashion at this outrageous allegation.

MR. F. It is not outrageous and I will prove it. Miss Malone you have been scratching yourself since you

20

entered the witness box. Do you deny it?

LILY I suppose I gave myself a few scratches alright but who doesn't?

MR. F. Why were you scratching?

LILY To get relief from the itching.

MR. F. But what made you itchy?

LILY It could be anything.

MR. F. Could it be fleas?

LILY I don't know.

MR. F. I would remind you Miss Malone that you are under oath.

JUDGE You will please answer the question.

LILY It was fleas but since our society's rules expressly forbid the killing of any of God's creatures it is an honour to carry fleas. The more fleas a member of the S.P.G.C. has on his or her person the higher the seat in heaven.

MR. F. But if you love fleas so deeply why do you scratch? Do you not know that the nail of a single finger is to a flea what a twenty foot iron bar is to a duman being. During your scratching you must have killed several fleas. In fact there is one part of your anatomy which you stopped scratching some minutes ago. I am prepared to wager that the entire flea population of that area has been scratched to death. Are there dead fleas on your person Miss Malone?

LILY I don't know.

MR. F. You will answer yes or no.

JUDGE I warn you that it is punishable by monetary fine to take up the time of the court. Answer the question.

LILY I suppose there are some dead ones.

MR. F. Then by all the powers that be you are a self-confessed murderess.

LILY It was purely accidental. Everyone does it.

MR. F. My lord I submit that this woman consciously and self-indulgently did so scratch her body that she must take full responsibility for the brutal murder of several fleas not to mention the mutilation of a great many

21

more. I further submit that a woman as inhuman and irresponsible as she who now faces us from the dock should not be taken seriously. I must therefore respectfully request that her evidence be eradicated from the court records.

JUDGE What you ask is impossible Mister Fog. I will certainly take note of what you say and I assure you that it will weigh heavily with me when passing sentence. You may step down Miss Malone. (*To Court Clerk*.) Have this woman apprehended and charged under the act.

(*The Court Clerk escorts Lily Malone from the court. She weeps distractedly*.)

JUDGE Has the prosecution further witnesses?

MR. C. No my lord.

JUDGE Mister Fog?

MR. F. I have but one witness my lord. She is Miss Mary O'Dorey the daughter of the accused.

JUDGE Call Mary O'Dorey.

CLERK Call Mary O'Dorey.

(*Enter Mary O'Dorey. She is a young and beautiful woman. She takes her place in the box and is sworn*.)

MR. F. You are Mary O'Dorey?

MARY Yes.

MR. F. You are the eldest child of John O'Dorey the defendant in this case?

MARY Yes.

MR. F. Have you many brothers and sisters?

MARY I have five brothers and seven sisters.

MR. F. How are you employed?

MARY I look after my father and my brothers and sisters.

MR. F. Why doesn't your mother do this?

MARY Because my mother is dead.

MR. F. (*For benefit of court*.) Oh . . . So your mother is dead.

MR. C. (*Rises*.) It must now be apparent to all that Mister Fog is up to his old tricks again. Here he is trying to win sympathy for the defendant, stooping to the basest tricks. My lord this court was convened so that evidence might be heard from reliable witnesses. It was not convened to listen to melodramatic sob stories.

MR. F. My lord I will show that this girl's evidence has a direct bearing on the case.

JUDGE Very well. Sit down Mister Crystal. Please proceed Mister Fog.

MR. F. How long is your mother dead?

MARY Two years.

MR. F. How did she die?

MARY She died in childbirth.

MR. C. Here we go again.

MR. F. Since your mother died how has your father behaved?

MARY He is the soul of kindness to all of us but he is distracted and absent-minded not knowing half the time what he is doing.

MR. F. Not knowing half the time what he was doing. Is that what you said?

MARY Yes.

MR. F. Should your father die what would happen to you and your brothers and sisters?

MARY I'm afraid we would starve if we didn't die of the heartbreak.

MR. F. On the seventh day of June, the day on which it is alleged your father dumped the sour goat's milk into the stream of Awnygilly how did he conduct himself?

MARY He was going around in a daze.

MR. F. A daze?

MARY In a tizzy.

MR. F. In a tizzy?

MARY Like he'd be drunk or something.

MR. F. And was he drunk?

MARY He didn't put a drink to his lips since my mother died.

MR. F. Anymore?

MARY He put on his trousers backwards. He put his shoes on the wrong feet. He stirred his tea with his spectacles

23

and buttered his bread with his pocket comb. He washed his pocket watch with a toothbrush and tried to wind his false teeth.

MR. F. Was there a reason for these absurd actions?

MARY It was the second anniversary of my poor mother's death.

MR. F. (*Looks around.*) Oh may God help us all. Oh woe, woe, woe. Would you say that your father did not know what he was going on that day?

MARY I would.

MR. F. This business of the sour milk. Have you anything to say regarding it?

MARY It was in the two gallon enamel bucket. There was only a pint or two and it was wanted for making pancakes. I promised the children I would make pancakes. I don't know what possessed my father to dump it, that's if he did dump it.

MR. F. Just now that's not the point. Would you say that your father was not in his right mind on the seventh of June?

MARY God help us sir he was demented and fiercely disturbed.

MR. F. Would you say he was not aware of his actions?

MARY Yes.

MR. F. Would you say that he did not know right from wrong?

MARY I would.

MR. F. Would you say he was what you country people call mental?

MARY Yes, he was mental.

MR. F. Thank you. (*To Crystal.*) Your witness.

MR. C. What age are you Miss O'Dorey?

MARY I'll be twenty on my next birthday.

MR. C. Then you would be old enough to remember the many times your father was in jail?

MARY Yes sir.

MR. C. The time he received the suspended sentence for

sneezing in Church . . . was he in his right mind then?

MARY I don't know sir.

MR. C. The time he was put away for dumping the date stones, the orange peel and the apple butts . . . was he what you country people would call mental?

MARY I don't know sir.

MR. C. If you don't answer yes or no I'll ask the judge to cite you for contempt of court. Was he mental when he dumped the orange peel?

MARY I suppose he wasn't.

MR. C. When he was convicted to eighteen months for public spitting was he mental?

MARY No.

MR. C. And was your mother alive on those occasions?

MARY She was.

MR. C. Then your father needs no extenuating circumstances to start him on a course of indiscriminate dumping.

MARY I suppose so sir.

MR. C. My lord I suggest that this man John O'Dorey has no redeeming feature whatsoever and in suggesting temporary derangement counsel for the defense is trying to hoodwink the court. This crime of O'Dorey's ranks with the lunatic defilement of the nineteen sixties, seventies and eighties when polluters stalked the beauty spots of the world destroying, raping, deflowering and defoliating.

MR. C. Hitler and his minions were innocents by comparison. Hitler was an uneducated psychopath but the industrialists of the last century were university graduates who knew what they were doing. I rank the defendant alongside of these murderers. Anything less than the death penalty would be a sin against mankind.

MARY Oh my poor father. They're going to kill my poor father. (*Weeps.*) We'll all be orphans.

JUDGE Remove her.

MARY Oh my poor brothers and sisters. Orphans every one of us without a father or a mother. Oh mother

of Jesus take pity. Oh God soften the hearts of judges.
(*She weeps as she is led from court.*)
(*Exit Mary.*)
(*Clerk returns to his position.*)

JUDGE Does prosecution or defense wish to recall any of the witnesses?

MR. C. No my lord.

JUDGE Mr. Fog?

MR. F. No my lord.

JUDGE It's a warm day.

FOG AND CRYSTAL Yes my lord.

JUDGE There have been many demands on us. I think an adjournment is in order.

FOG AND CRYSTAL Yes my lord.

JUDGE I'll adjourn 'till two o'clock. On resumption I will hear final submissions. After that will come the summing-up.

MR. F. I would like an adjournment of twenty four hours if it so please the court.

JUDGE So would I but it simply cannot be done.

MR. F. My client's life hangs in the balance.

JUDGE Medical evidence now clearly shows that unless capital crimes are tried in a matter of hours the ensuing stress is damaging for everybody. I am sorry Mister Fog.

MR. FOG. Give me 'till eight o'clock.

JUDGE I have a dinner appointment at eight o'clock.

MR. FOG Very well my lord. I have done my best. I can do no more.

JUDGE After the final submissions and the summing up I will pass sentence. Clerk!

CLERK Yes my lord.

JUDGE (*Takes some change from pocket.*) Be a good fellow. Find a decent draper's shop and get me a good quality black cap. Size eight.
(*Lights out*).

Lights up. Two o'clock. Same place. All are present save the Judge and the Clerk of the court. Mr. F. (To

*Mister Crystal. having looked at his watch): * She's late.

MR. C. She's always late. What do you think?

MR. F. Toss of a coin.

MR. C. You haven't a hope.

MR. F. So you say. Luckily for us you're not judging here.

MR. C. That's because I voted wrong. Next time I'll vote right.

MR. F. You could be wrong again.

MR. C. We'll see. One thing is sure. Your man needn't worry about the price of bacon from now on.

JOHN Is he talking about me?

MR. F. You mustn't take any notice of him.

JOHN If it comes to the worst will you do what you can for my children?

MR. F. Now, now, you're jumping your fences before you come to them.

JOHN I meant no harm. I never did anything deliberate.

MR. C. My friend I fear you are a refugee from the nineteen seventies. In those days crimes like yours were ignored, even condoned by most authorities. The truth is you don't belong in this day and age.

JOHN It looks as if I won't belong long more.

MR. F. Now, now, that's no way to talk.

MR. C. It won't hurt you. You won't feel anything.

JOHN What's it like?

MR. C. The clerk of the court will spray you with a mortification mixture. Death is instant and according to the manufacturers quite painless. Of course, you know manufacturers. Then when you're stiff they'll stuff you in a furnace.

JOHN Dear God I hope it doesn't come to that.

MR. C. You never know your luck. Still I wouldn't count on any leniency. If you ask me you're bloody lucky to be getting out of this damned nightmare. I wish I was in your place. I have a blasted wife and she's a caution. Never a day's peace.

JOHN I'll gladly swap places with you.

MR. C. Are you a barrister?

JOHN No.

MR. C. Then it's fundamentally impossible and legally unacceptable.

JOHN I'm terrified at the thoughts of dying.

MR. F. You're too pessimistic. You're not dead yet.

MR. C. I wouldn't worry. We'll all have to go sooner or later.

(*Enter the Clerk of the court.*)

CLERK All stand.

(*All stand.*)

(*Enter the Judge. She takes her place on bench. Clerk sits. All sit.*)

JUDGE (*To Fog.*) Where did you have lunch Walter?

MR. F. At the Self Service.

JUDGE What was it like?

MR. F. Pretty good. (*Indicates John.*) Your man here didn't eat much. I had mushroom soup for openers and cutlets for the main course. Price was reasonable.

JUDGE Mine was bloody awful. I went to that new hotel. I made the fatal mistake of ordering stew. God Almighty it would turn your stomach. How 'bout you Barney?

MR. C. My sister in law's married to the M.O. here. I had lunch with them. They laid it on, roast duck, orange sauce, the lot.

JUDGE I'll bring a pack lunch and a flask of soup in future. Let's get this thing over with. I'll hear final submissions.

MR. C. My lord I do not propose to keep this court sitting for any longer than is strictly necessary. The defendant John O'Dorey is without doubt guilty of the crime with which he is charged. The excuse that his mind was elsewhere at the time is nothing but a downright lie. My mind is often elsewhere and so is yours my lord but we do not commit capital crimes. Once a lawabiding citizen always a lawabiding citizen. Habit dies hard. This man is a habitual dumper and yet he

28

knows the law in respect of dumping. Nothing may be dumped without prior inspection by a registered analyst.

JOHN I have no money for analysts.

JUDGE You will not interrupt sir. Pray proceed Mr. Crystal.

MR. C. The long trail of havoc and destruction underneath the ripples of the Awnygilly stream is this man's major contribution to the further evolution of mankind. He has clearly shown himself to be no respector of life. Therefore, he is not deserving of life. Only those who respect life are deserving of it. Man has never been given a mandate to kill another of God's creatures. Calculated killing is one of the great enemies of natural evolution. Many wonderful species of life have disappeared from this planet because in less enlightened times man believed that he was within his rights to kill other creatures for pleasure or for food. God gave him no such right. The fifth commandment says thou shalt not kill. Man in his ignorance understood this to mean it was alright to kill other creatures. If God meant this to be so he would have told Moses and Moses would have inscribed it on the tablet. All we find on the tablet is thou shalt not kill and this clearly means thou shalt not kill anything, let it be fish, flesh, fowl or good red herring. Man may kill in self defence but only in the direst extremity. In conclusion my lord let me point out that man today is wreaking his own destruction, not all men, (*Points to Dorey*) this man and a few others like him. Are we all to be sentenced to death because of this capricious wretch or is God still in his heaven to see that justice is done, to see that this monster and his equals are wiped off the face of the earth. I appreciate the indulgence of the court. (*He sits.*)

JUDGE You may begin Mister Fog.

MR. F. Not having dined as well as Mister Crystal I will make no attempt to match his eloquence. My lord, my client John O'Dorey is a simple unlettered man and the sole support of a large family. His wife is dead and John has not been himself since she was taken from him. These are the simple facts of the case. He has made no attempt to deny having dumped the goat's milk. There can be no doubt that he was not in his right mind when he did so. There has been no attempt at evasion or duplicity. He has been a frank and open witness and his ready testimony has hastened the business of the court. You have seen his daughter. She is a beautiful young woman. All his children are pure and beautiful. It is a hard man who would find it in his heart to deprive them of the father they love so deeply. John O'Dorey did not kill deliberately. Therefore, he should never have been charged with murder. Manslaughter or rather creature slaughter would be a fairer charge. My colleague spoke awhile ago of evolution. If there is one great accomplishment emerging from man's evolution surely that accomplishment is charity. The amount of charity shown by this court on this afternoon should be a fair criterion of how far man has really evolved, how far he has removed himself from the shadow of the great apes who were his brothers. Acquit this poor backward fellow my lord and show the world that man is the noblest of all God's creatures. . . . Prove for once and for all time my lord that man, because he is capable of charity, is nearer to God than the beasts of the fields, the birds of the air and the fishes of the sea. Let it be shown through your clemency that man deserves to survive all forms of contamination and pollution because he was possessed of the fortitude to relieve the anguish in other human souls and to extend his charity to other human hearts.

My lord return this man this day to the home and the children he loves and let the word go abroad to every place that man is not yet shorn of love, of decency and of dignity. I thank you my lord.

(*He sits.*)

JUDGE I must say gentlemen that you are both outstanding credits to the bar. I have been moved and impressed in turn by each of you. You have simplified my task and made points I would have overlooked.

FOR AND CRYSTAL Thank you my lord.

JUDGE Will the accused take his place in the dock.

CLERK Come along please.

(*Clerk shows Dorey to dock. Returns to his seat.*)

JUDGE I will do my humble best to sum up and assess. Gentlemen it must be said at once that the species known as homo sapiens was without natural enemy till the birth of pollution. That is why pollution must rank as the greatest crime of all time and that is why there can be no leniency shown to those convicted of such a crime. To show leniency would be to stifle the cry of the newborn babe and to contaminate the milk in the breast of it's mother.

I have no doubt whatsoever that John O'Dorey dumped sour goat's milk from an enamel bucket into the stream of Awnygilly thereby causing the numerous deaths described earlier. It is possible, although I am not conceding this, that he did not dump it deliberately. The fact is that by his action he was responsible for mass murder.

It reflects on him that he should perpetrate such a monstrous crime at a time when our government is spending billions to arrest the spread of pollution. There are constant radio and television campaigns, daily warnings in the newspapers, notices outside every church, school and police station, all aimed at the John O'Doreys of this world. I can find no excuse for his wanton disregard of such timely warnings. The man shows himself to be a fully qualified scoundrel without regard of any kind for the welfare of his neighbours.

One can forgive in part the savage stupidity of the nineteen seventies when with an ignorance and lunatic abandon unparalled in recorded history allegedly mature human beings dumped gigantic tankers of filth and refuse into our streams and rivers, destroying many forms of life with poisonous discharges, turning our seas and lakes into steaming cesspools. We must forget the deeds of these criminals who walked the streets as free men and who blighted the human race to its final generation. Would I could go back in time to curse the craven cowards of the nineteen seventies who knew what was happening but who thought only of themselves. The magnitude of their crime against future generations will never be fully measured. We must forgive and try to forget but . . . one cannot forgive in this day and age. The cost, in terms of human life, would be monumental. John O'Dorey has shown himself to be a danger to humanity and a threat to the lives of all of us. I would be shirking my duty if I were to make light of his crime. I will now pronounce sentence.

CLERK Will the prisoner stand.

(*O'Dorey stands.*)

(*Judge produces a black cap which she dons.*)

JOHN (*Screams.*) Oh no. God pity me, my children . . . Jesus help me. . . . (*He almost collapses. He sobs brokenly.*)

JUDGE John O'Dorey I sentence you to death by spraying. (*Dorey moans and sobs uncontrollably.*)

JUDGE The clerk will see that the sentence is carried out without delay.

(*Whistling industriously the Clerk locates an elaborate spraying machine and stands in front of the dock.*)

JUDGE (*To Dorey.*) May the lord have mercy on your immortal soul.

(*Dorey draws himself upward and stands manfully to face his executioner.*)

JUDGE Let him be sprayed.

CLERK He shall be sprayed.

(*The Clerk sprays the head and shoulders of John O'Dorey. Dorey shudders, wilts and collapses. All cross themselves. The Clerk goes into dock to examine John.)*

JUDGE Is he dead?

CLERK Dead as a doornail my lord.

JUDGE Amen say I. Where does a decent girl go for a drink in this town?

MR. F. Mr. Crystal and I will be having a few later if you would care to join us.

JUDGE I'd love that. (*To Clerk of court*) That will be all.

CLERK Yes my lord.

JUDGE You'll come round later when rigor mortis sets in. Better check on the furnaces before you leave.

CLERK Yes my lord. My lord?

JUDGE What is it now?

CLERK Beg permission to keep his clothes and shoes.

JUDGE Oh very well. Get along with you now.

(Clerk obsequiously bows himself out. Exit clerk. As barristers gather together the last of their papers Judge produces a small compact and examines herself in mirror. Barristers join her.)

MR. C. Ready my lord.

JUDGE Ready. Before we go Barney there's a question I'd like to ask. This concerns you too Walter. Please be honest with me.

MR. F. I'll try.

MR. C. Let's have it.

JUDGE This cap? Do you think it suits me?

MR. C. By Jove it does. It certainly does.

MR. F. It does something for you alright.

JUDGE In that case I think I'll leave it on. Lets go.

(Exit all three.)

CURTAIN.

BACKWATER

A play in one act.

CHARACTERS IN ORDER OF APPEARANCE:

JIMMY SWAN

SAMMY FURLONG

EDDIE DOYLE

MRS. MARY SWAN

The sitting room of a middle-class home in the village of Fongo in the southwest of Ireland. The time is the evening of a July day of the present time. The sitting room is empty of people. It has all the trappings of a previous generation; old suite of furniture, sideboard, china cabinet etcetera. From the mantle an old clock rings out the hour of eight. There is a brief silence. Then suddenly the door bursts open and a young man enters. He carries a large suitcase which he deposits on the floor. He looks round the room and walks about fingering and fondling objects as he finds them. This man is Jimmy Swan. Suddenly he goes to door by which he entered.

JIMMY Come on in lads.
   (*Enter two men, one the same age as Jimmy. He too has a suitcase. His name is Sammy Furlong. The other man is older, maybe forty. He is hesitant about entering. He carries a suitcase. He is Eddie Doyle.*)
JIMMY For God's sake move in from the door Eddie. We're not burglars. This is my home we're in.
   (*Sheepsshly Eddie moves into room. Jimmy puts all the suitcases to one side.*)

JIMMY This place hasn't changed. There isn't an item out of place.

SAMMY How long exactly has it been Jimmy?

JIMMY Exactly? Exactly it's been nine years and two months.

SAMMY That's a long time.

JIMMY Well that's what it's been. She was standing right where you are now Eddie and I here. There were tears in her eyes, in mine too. I kissed her and said no more, just walked out without looking around. It had to be done that way, a quick, sudden break, no lingering.

SAMMY You think she'll be annoyed. It's so long.

JIMMY My mother? No. She'll be glad to see me. I know my mother.

SAMMY You may be expecting too much after nine years.

JIMMY I'm her only son remember. She has nobody else.

EDDIE Do you think she'll have any objection to us.

JIMMY Why should she. You're my friends.

EDDIE Maybe you should have written and told her.

JIMMY It's better this way. If I wrote and told her there's no end to the trouble she'd have gone to. Painting, papering, polishing and the devil knows what.

EDDIE Still . . . walking in on top of her like this without warning . . .

JIMMY You worry too much Eddie. Wait till you meet her. All your worries will be over.

SAMMY Seems a lively little village.

JIMMY That's only for the carnival. It's a dreadful back-water the rest of the year.

EDDIE Still it's a pretty place. Fine river and plenty trees. Mountains as well, not too far off. I can't remember when I've seen a place as nice.

JIMMY Oh it's as nice as any. I'll grant you that. What used to kill me was the boredom.

SAMMY Well it isn't boring now.

JIMMY I keep telling you that's because of the carnival. The pubs have an extension and there are football matches. There's a donkey derby. There's a marquee for dancing and you saw the amusements' park from the bus but it's only for ten days. Then the place becomes a graveyard again. That's why I chose this particular period to come. I just couldn't endure it any other time.

EDDIE I don't know. It's the sort of place that appeals to me. Nice and peaceful. That's a good-looking river. If there's one thing I love it's a quiet inland place.

JIMMY You weren't born here. You never spent a winter here. The girls get out when they're eighteen.

SAMMY And the boys follow?

JIMMY Most of them do. A few stay and rot.

SAMMY Same everywhere isn't it?

JIMMY I don't know. I can only speak for this place. I love my mother of course but a man has to spread out and look at the world.

EDDIE Is London the world?

JIMMY I knew you'd come up with one like that. I've been to more places than London Eddie and you know it.

EDDIE Of course you have. I shouldn't have asked.

JIMMY That's alright. By the way my mother knows all about you two. The seldom time I write I give you a mention.

SAMMY Then we're not complete strangers.

EDDIE There's one thing I want to make clear now Jimmy. If we stay here we pay out way, at least Sammy and me.

JIMMY I'll fix all that.

EDDIE Let us have our way in this one. It's what we want.

SAMMY Eddie's right Jimmy.

JIMMY Why not wait till you're leaving and then give her a present.

EDDIE Fair enough.

SAMMY That's reasonable.

EDDIE That's a good idea when you think on it.

JIMMY Come on and I'll show you where you can freshen

up. (*Leads them to another door.*) Go right up the stairs. It's there at the top of the landing.

(*Exit Sammy.*)

EDDIE You're sure your mother won't take a dim view of us?

JIMMY She'll be delighted. This is Fongo Carnival. She'll love the company. Everybody goes gay during the carnival. Don't worry.

EDDIE Whatever you say. (*Exit Eddie.*)

(*Jimmy returns and lifts his suitcase on to the table. He opens it and takes out a neatly wrapped package. He closes suitcase and returns it to original position. He places the package on the mantle. He takes a music box from the mantle and lifts the cover. A tinny nostalgic tune can be heard. Meanwhile a figure appears at the first entrance. It is Jimmy Swan's mother Mary. She carries a bag of messages.*)

MRS. SWAN (*Tentatively*) Jimmy? (*Jimmy doesn't hear her.*)

MRS. SWAN Jimmy? Oh Jimmy. Oh my son. (*They embrace.*)

JIMMY Mother. It's good to see you.

MRS. SWAN Oh Jimmy. It's been so long. Nine years and never a visit.

JIMMY I often meant to come. I really did mother but something always cropped up. Once as I was on the point of leaving I got the bloody flu and another time I hurt my leg. There was always some damned thing. There was last Christmas. My ticket was bought and paid for and I was all set to come. Got this bloody nose bleed. Had to see a doctor. Said I'd be mad to travel.

MRS. SWAN Nine years. Oh Jimmy how could you. All the lonely Christmas times I've spent. All the long days and nights. There was one winter I spent two weeks in bed. I was there three days helpless before anybody knew about it.

JIMMY I'm sorry mother, I really am. It was mostly bad

luck that prevented me. I swear I was ready ten times when some damned thing happened. I'm so sorry.

MRS. SWAN I know you are Jimmy. I know and I know you meant well but it was hard. Men are so heedless most of the time. I only want you to know what it was like.

JIMMY It won't happen again.

MRS. SWAN It doesn't matter anymore. Have you had something to eat?

JIMMY Oh sure. We had a meal before boarding the bus.

MRS. SWAN We? Is there somebody with you?

JIMMY A few pals. They've gone upstairs for a wash. I've got a present for you. (*Takes package from mantle.*) It's a shawl. I had my landlady get it. (*He busily unwraps package.*) It cost a packet I can tell you. She had to order it specially. It's hand-crocheted whatever that means. I told her to spare no expense. What do you think?

(*Mrs. Swan accepts shawl.*)

MRS. SWAN It's beautiful. You shouldn't have spent so much.

JIMMY Oh that's nothing.

MRS. SWAN I should have thanked you for the money you sent.

JIMMY Sorry it wasn't more often.

MRS. SWAN There are some who never send any. I'm grateful.

JIMMY This time when I get back I'll be more regular. I'll come home more often too, twice a year, summer and Christmas. That's a promise.

MRS. SWAN Yes Jimmy.

JIMMY I mean it mother. I know how you must have felt. It must have been terrible for you.

MRS. SWAN It was too long a time. A person hardens up inside. A person has to, to avoid being hurt again. It's just a matter of protecting oneself. Then there were the neighbours. At first they used to ask how you were doing. After a year they stopped asking.

They thought it would embarrass me. I used to cry a lot over you. The first years I used to cry all the time because I gave you no cause not to come home to me. A person has only so many tears . . . I had to accustom myself to being without you.

JIMMY Oh God I'm sorry mother. I never realised what it must have been like for you.

MRS. SWAN (*Adjusting herself.*) It's alright. Tell me about your friends.

JIMMY They're two chaps I work with. We share the same digs.

MRS. SWAN Will they be staying?

JIMMY If it's alright with you.

MRS. SWAN You know it is. How long?

JIMMY We have a fortnight.

MRS. SWAN That's nice. 'Twill be a change to have company.

JIMMY I'd better give you some money. (*He extracts wallet and hands her a number of bank notes.*)

MRS. SWAN Can you afford all this. It seems such a lot.

JIMMY It's nothing.

MRS. SWAN I wouldn't take it but things are so dear.

JIMMY The boys wanted to chip in but they agreed that it would be better to do something when they're leaving.

MRS. SWAN Are they decent boys Jimmy?

JIMMY Oh yes. Definitely although there's one of them and you'd hardly call him a boy. I'm sure he's over forty.

MRS. SWAN So long as they're decent men I don't care.

JIMMY I've known them for years now and I honestly couldn't say a single word against either one of them.

MRS. SWAN The carnival opened last night. The village was packed.

JIMMY Seems like another big turn-out tonight. The crowds were gathering as we came in. I wonder what would the village of Fongo be like without it's carnival?

MRS. SWAN I imagine we'd miss it at first and be disappointed. Then we'd grow used to it the way we do to every other disappointment.

JIMMY Yes I see. I think my pals are coming. You'll like these fellows mother. We've been mates a long time.

(*Enter Sammy Furlong.*)

JIMMY I want you to meet my mother Sammy. This is my friend Sammy Furlong mother, one of the best.

MRS. SWAN Sammy. (*Shakes hands.*) You're welcome.

SAMMY Thank you Mrs. Swan.

JIMMY An this is Eddie Doyle. For God's sake come away from the door Eddie. It's only my mother. There's none shyer than this fellow.

(*Eddie comes forward shyly and accepts Mrs. Swan's hand.*)

MRS. SWAN You're welcome Eddie. I hope you'll have a nice stay here.

(*Eddie nods by way of appreciation*).

MRS. SWAN Jimmy tells me you boys have eaten a while ago. It's no trouble to prepare something if you're hungry.

SAMMY No thank you. We couldn't look at food. Unless Eddie . . . you want something?

EDDIE No thanks. I'm full.

JIMMY Look why don't the three of you sit down a minute. I'll take your bags up. I won't be a jiffy.

(*He locates suitcases.*) Eddie will tell you the story of his life while I'm gone.

(*Jimmy and Sammy laugh at this. Exit Jimmy with two suitcases.*)

MRS. SWAN Please sit down. I hope you don't mind sharing a room.

SAMMY Not at all.

EDDIE I hope it's alright?

MRS. SWAN Oh?

EDDIE Our staying here I mean.

MRS. SWAN You're most welcome, all of you.

SAMMY It's good for you to have us Mrs. Swan. We

weren't sure what with Jimmy not letting you know we were coming and all.

MRS. SWAN Jimmy can be thoughtless but he's a good boy really.

SAMMY No better.

MRS. SWAN He told me you stay at the same lodgings.

SAMMY That's right. The Kilburn High Road.

MRS. SWAN I know the address. Is it alright?

SAMMY Oh yes. It's good enough. Landlady's Irish. She's married with her own family but we fit in nicely. The grub's alright and it's clean. That's the important thing.

MRS. SWAN Who does your laundry?

SAMMY It's collected.

MRS. SWAN Are you far from the church?

SAMMY Just a couple of blocks. Got Irish priests and all.

MRS. SWAN It must be like home then.

EDDIE No. It's not like home.

SAMMY I like it. I wouldn't live here now if I got a fortune. Jimmy's the same.

EDDIE No he's not. It's just that the money's so good.

SAMMY That's what I meant. Seriously that's what I meant Mrs. Swan.

EDDIE If he could get a decent job he'd be back in the morning.

MRS. SWAN Thank you. Is the work hard?

SAMMY Work is easy. Hours are long if you want to make the big money. Jimmy and I work overtime for the beer money.

MRS. SWAN Do you drink Mr. Doyle?

SAMMY Not him. He saves his money. Oh he'll have a drink or two the weekend but you won't catch him drinking no rake of beer. He says he's got to think of the rainy day. Me and Jimmy expect the weather to stay fine awhile yet. Easy come, easy go Mrs. Swan.

MRS. SWAN Is your mother alive Mr. Furlong?

SAMMY Don't know. I never seen her.

MRS. SWAN Oh.

EDDIE Sammy was reared in an English orphanage.

41

MRS. SWAN Oh.

SAMMY I used have an auntie come and visit me only she wasn't a real aunt. She used come and take me out days, once for a week-end. A lot of the boys had aunties. Mine was an old lady who worked in a library. She didn't really like me but it was good for her. I think her doctor recommended it. She's dead now. It wasn't too bad. The nuns had no favourites. I'll say that for them.

MRS. SWAN Did you not ever think of marrying?

SAMMY (*Laughs.*) Now why would you want me to go and do a bloody awful thing like that. I never done you no harm.

MRS. SWAN Some day some nice girl will come along and you'll see. . . .

SAMMY Oh she'll come along alright and I'll see alright. That way I'll be able to duck.

MRS. SWAN What about you Mr. Doyle? Are your parents alive?

EDDIE They're both dead.

SAMMY His father was drowned.

MRS. SWAN Oh I'm sorry.

SAMMY He was a fisherman. Eddie used to fish too but he jacked it up.

MRS. SWAN I daresay the sea's alright for pleasure but it's a different matter when you have to make a living out of it.

EDDIE The sea's a cruel mistress. I never liked her. I like quiet places inland where the water's fresh and predictable.

MRS. SWAN I know what you mean.

EDDIE Just looking at water will suit me fine from now on.

MRS. SWAN Did you not ever think of getting married?

EDDIE Yes. I thought of it. But somehow I just could never seem to get going in that direction. It's a wonder you never married again?

MRS. SWAN Who'd have me?

EDDIE You'd be surprised.

MRS. SWAN Oh go on. I'm so used to being alone now that I just couldn't be bothered.

SAMMY How long's your husband dead?

MRS. SWAN Twenty five years. Just after Jimmy was born.

EDDIE I'm amazed you never married again.

MRS. SWAN In a backwater like this you'd hardly get an offer in a lifetime.

EDDIE In your case that could never be true.

MRS. SWAN Oh its true. You'd have to live here to find out how true it is.

SAMMY Why didn't you leave?

MRS. SWAN I often meant to but when the time came I found my roots had gone in too deep. My husband's buried here.

SAMMY But that's such a long time ago.

MRS. SWAN Yes it is but you're too young yet to appreciate how roots can hold a person.

SAMMY Maybe I'll find out some day.

MRS. SWAN If you settle down you will. I'm quite content the way I am now. Sunday nights I play Bingo in the parish hall. In the winter the fit-ups come every few weeks. Then there's Christmas and Saint Patrick's Day and Easter. The year is nicely broken up between everything. In the summer there's the carnival. There's always something really. The walks are nice especially in the spring and autumn. It all depends I suppose on what a person wants.

EDDIE It sounds a great life to me.

SAMMY I don't know. I think I'd go out of my mind between walking and the Bingo. It's definitely not for me. Give me the Crown in Cricklewood. Give me Pickadill of a Saturday night. Gimme any part of London any time. That's where the life is. You don't have to beg for nothing in London.

EDDIE That's true. It's like Mrs. Swan just said . . . it all depends on what a person wants. I don't want the same as you nor Sammy doesn't want the same as me. The tough part is that not all people get

43

what they want. I suppose that's as it should be. If a man wants something simple and good most likely he can have it in due course but if he wants too much he may end up by getting nothing at all.

MRS. SWAN Here's Jimmy. (*Enter Jimmy.*)

JIMMY Well I'm all set.

SAMMY That's a good job and all. Where's the nearest boozer.

JIMMY Right next door.

SAMMY That's downright thoughtful, that is.

JIMMY Don't wait up for us mother. We're really going to do the town.

SAMMY How many pubs is there then?

JIMMY There's three all told.

SAMMY Good Christ.

JIMMY Hard to credit isn't it.

SAMMY If it wasn't yourself told me I wouldn't have believed it. You got a Lord Mayor then, a council and all that?

JIMMY No but we got the electric light. You turn on this tiny little switch 'bout the size o' your belly button and the whole place lights up same as if 'twas day.

SAMMY Go on, you're pulling my leg.

JIMMY So help me. You ever hear of a fridge. (*Sammy shakes his head.*) You get a saucer and fill it with water. Put it in the fridge and wait an hour. When you take it out the water's turned to ice.

SAMMY Next thing you'll tell me is you got wirelesses, you know . . . them boxes that sings and talks. . . .

EDDIE Alright you two. That's enough clowning. (*To Mrs. Swan.*) They're always at that sort of thing. It comes from being too much in the city.

MRS. SWAN I don't mind.

SAMMY What are we waiting for then? You right Jimmy?

JIMMY I'm rearin' to go.

SAMMY You right Eddie?

EDDIE You're not going without your mother?

JIMMY (*Laughs.*) My mother never goes to the pub.

44

MRS. SWAN I might go if I was asked.

JIMMY But you never. . . .

MRS. SWAN This is carnival time.

JIMMY Oh God mother I'm sorry. I'd love to have you with us. I really would. It just didn't occur to me.

MRS. SWAN You go on, the three of you. Maybe I'll pop out later.

JIMMY You go right upstairs and change this minute.

SAMMY None of us is leaving here till you come down.

MRS. SWAN I'll come later. That's a promise. I've got some shopping to do. You'll want breakfasts in the morning and you'll want your meals. I've got beds to make. Now go along and I'll be out in an hour or so. You're on holidays. I want you to enjoy yourselves. Go on. Off with you now.

(*She shoos them towards door.*)

JIMMY You'll come for sure.

MRS. SWAN I promise.

SAMMY If you don't I'm coming back here for you. I'll bloody well abduct you.

MRS. SWAN The sooner you go the sooner I can start to get things done.

JIMMY Alright then. We'll see you in an hour.

(*Exit Jimmy and Sammy.*)

MRS. SWAN I seldom go in the pubs. When my husband was alive I might go now and again with him but only during the carnival.

EDDIE Of course. In case the boys grow tired of waiting and want to visit the other pubs I'll hang on next door.

MRS. SWAN There's no need. It won't be hard to find them in Fongo.

EDDIE I don't mind. I like to stay in one place.

(*Exit Eddie.*)

LIGHTS FADE OUT.

Night time a week later. Enter Mrs. Swan followed by Eddie.

MRS. SWAN If I take more than two drinks my head begins to spin and I don't know where I am. At a party last Christmas I drank four sherries and I nearly passed out. Would you like a cup of tea Mr. Doyle?

EDDIE No thank you. It keeps me awake. I haven't drunk so much since my twenty first birthday. Still I enjoyed the night. The boys were in their element.

MRS. SWAN Are they like that in London Mr. Doyle?

EDDIE Why don't you call me Eddie. I'm not used to being called mister. It sort of embarrasses me.

MRS. SWAN Then you call me Mary.

EDDIE I'd like that. To answer your question, they cut it up on week-ends alright. But otherwise no.

MRS. SWAN Why don't you sit down Eddie.

EDDIE Alright, if you will.

MRS. SWAN You're sure there's nothing you'd like. Maybe a glass of milk.

EDDIE No. I don't think so. Sit down and tell me about the village.

MRS. SWAN There's nothing special about it. There are three hundred people give or take a few. There's the church and the school and if you're looking for excitement there's the carnival.

(They both laugh.)

EDDIE Go on.

MRS. SWAN Nothing much happens. Somebody dies. There's a marriage and somebody new comes into the world.

EDDIE Jimmy used to say the place was dying.

MRS. SWAN No. That's not so. It may seem like that to younger people or to those who don't look beneath the surface. The truth is the village is sleepy. The people are happy. They really are. There is great love between the couples and the children are fresh and innocent. It's only when they go away that they change for the worse. It's a good place. Everybody has enough. I doubt if anybody has more than enough but what does one want. Do you want to be flying around all the time seeking new pleasures, if you could call them that, or do you want to enjoy the simple pleasures that are to be found by reaching out your hand. I think my life here is happier than most. It's lonely sometimes but it doesn't hurt anymore. People just don't know where real pleasure lies, where true happiness can be found.

EDDIE I've only spent a week here and already I love the place. I've seen a lot of things I like. The village folk are friendly and easy going. There's so little noise. You know yesterday was the first time I heard a cock crow in twenty years.

MRS. SWAN I can see you like it here. The other two are beginning to get impatient. Only for the carnival they wouldn't endure it for more than a day.

EDDIE I could stay forever.

MRS. SWAN Surely you can't mean that.

EDDIE It's the truth.

MRS. SWAN But there must be thousands of villages like this. Surely there are quiet hamlets in England, peaceful places with friendly people.

EDDIE I'm not saying there aren't. I suppose when you come to think of it there must be places which are even prettier. If you want to know the chief reason I like this place is because you live here.

MRS. SWAN You can't mean that.

EDDIE I do.

MRS. SWAN But you hardly know me.

EDDIE That's where you're wrong. Ever since I met Jimmy five years ago I've known you. He had your photograph propped up on his dressing table—you and Jimmy on his Con firmation Day.

MRS. SWAN I remember that one.

EDDIE Well he showed it to us and even then, that first

time, I saw something in your face that made me want to come here.

MRS. SWAN I wish you wouldn't talk like that. I don't know what to say.

EDDIE Don't say anything. Anyway I held on to the photograph a good while and when he put his wallet back he forgot to ask me for it. So I kept it and every so often for th past five years I look at it. I suppose you could say I stole it. I never stole anything else in my life. I never saw anything worth stealing.

MRS. SWAN Oh now . . .

EDDIE It's the truth. I'm not good at chatting up women.

MRS. SWAN Did you never have a girl.

EDDIE Yes. Once.

MRS. SWAN She must have been special. Otherwise you wouldn't be able to say such thoughtful things.

EDDIE She was special.

MRS. SWAN She's dead isn't she.

EDDIE Yes.

MRS. SWAN Did you love her?

EDDIE Yes.

MRS. SWAN I'm sorry.

EDDIE It's all over now, just a memory.

MRS. SWAN Am I like her?

EDDIE Yes.

MRS. SWAN Ah then, that's the reason you kept the photograph.

EDDIE No.

MRS. SWAN It has to be.

EDDIE It isn't. The reason I kept the photograph was that I fell in love with you. I never thought I'd be saying this to you. It's like a dream. It's almost unreal.

MRS. SWAN You can't love a photograph.

EDDIE You can love a person in a photograph.

MRS. SWAN But I'm older than you. Ten years at least.

EDDIE We both know that makes no difference.

MRS. SWAN I don't know what to say.

EDDIE I still have the photograph. (*He produces his*

wallet and extracts photograph. He hands it to her.)

MRS. SWAN I've aged since then.

EDDIE Only a little.

MRS. SWAN You know nothing about me.

EDDIE I know all I need to know.

(*She returns photograph.*)

EDDIE Will you consider my proposal?

MRS. SWAN I can't think. You've taken me completely by surprise. It's too unexpected. I'm totally unprepared for such a thing. I couldn't consider it just now.

EDDIE Don't you even like me?

MRS. SWAN You must know Eddie the past few days have meant an awful lot to me. You've been so kind. Nobody's ever been so kind to me.

EDDIE I didn't do much for you.

MRS. SWAN It was you who got Jimmy to come home wasn't it?

EDDIE You can't make a person do something unless he wants to.

MRS. SWAN But it was you suggested it.

EDDIE Nobody forced him to come.

MRS. SWAN He'd never have come but for you. You put it into his head.

EDDIE He came because he wanted to.

MRS. SWAN It was you. I should have known.

EDDIE Please don't let it upset you.

MRS. SWAN To think that my own son for whom I made every sacrifice would never come to see me again but for the intercession of a stranger.

EDDIE Now, now, that's not true.

MRS. SWAN Oh God the world is a hard and stony place. I thought I was beyond hurt from that boy of mine. (*She starts to Cry.*)

EDDIE I wish you wouldn't cry.

MRS. SWAN The world is such that there's no one secure from hurt. What's it all for, the care and the rearing and the worrying. It makes no difference in the end.

Imagine to be dying with no word from him, from my one and only. The cruelty of it.

EDDIE Please don't cry. (*He places a hand on her shoulder.*) It's not as bad as it seems. (*He kneels by her side. He takes her hand. He holds it in his.*)

EDDIE I'll be here . . . No matter what I'll be here. You must never again feel that you'll be alone.

LIGHTS FADE OUT.

Night time a week later. Seated at table are Jimmy and Sammy. On the table are several beer bottles, some empty, some full. Sammy and Jimmy have partly filled glasses of beer in front of them.

SAMMY Well it's back to dear old Blighty in the morning.

JIMMY First thing when I get back I'm going down Soho for a girl.

SAMMY I'm going to the Crown. I want to see the crowd, hear the crack. It won't be long now.

JIMMY It can't be soon enough for me.

SAMMY Still it wasn't too bad while the carnival was on. At least the boozers were full and there was a singsong. Now there's nobody. Where's Eddie? You'd think he'd be in bed tonight. Bus leaves at seven in the morning.

JIMMY Didn't I tell you? He's gone to the Bingo with my mother.

SAMMY They've been having a right old time, haven't they.

JIMMY A Right old time? What's that supposed to mean?

SAMMY You know. Going for those walks together and now the Bingo.

JIMMY I don't see how that could be called a right old time by any stretch of the imagination.

SAMMY Sorry.

JIMMY A right old time could mean almost anything.

SAMMY I said I was sorry.

JIMMY It's highly suggestive.

50

SAMMY I think you're jealous.

JIMMY Jealous of who?

SAMMY Of Eddie.

JIMMY Knock it off will you. If you ask me the beer is gone to your head.

SAMMY You don't like the idea of his courting your mother.

JIMMY Courting? Did you say courting. You're mad.

SAMMY What else do you call it when a chap takes a woman out walking, when he takes her to the Bingo and then all the time they spend talking and gesturing and bloody well whispering. I don't know what you call it but I call it courting.

JIMMY My mother's too old for that caper. He's just a companion. It'll be all over tomorrow.

SAMMY Just like that?

JIMMY Just like that.

SAMMY What you mean is you hope 'twill be all over tomorrow.

JIMMY The three of us are going back to England first thing tomorrow morning. That's been agreed all the time.

SAMMY Suppose he asks your mother to come back with us.

JIMMY I know my mother. She'd never leave here.

SAMMY But suppose he does. Just suppose.

JIMMY You're reading all sorts of things into a casual relationship. What the hell's the matter with you anyway. Here we are nice and happy, getting slowly sozzled when you try to muck things up with your stupid talk about my mother and Eddie.

SAMMY It's not stupid talk and if you weren't my best friend I wouldn't bother. Why should I? All I'm trying to tell you is that there's something going on. You don't know it because you can't see the wood for the trees. It's different with me. I'm an outsider and I see things. As your friend I'm tipping you off.

JIMMY You mean there's something serious going on.

51

SAMMY At last you're getting the message.

JIMMY I don't believe it.

SAMMY Then don't. I could be wrong. All I want to do is get you ready in case of any surprise move. Eddie's a deep one.

JIMMY Don't I know.

SAMMY There is no part of the Irish Sea as deep as our Eddie.

JIMMY You're sure there's more to it than just knocking about together.

SAMMY I'm sure of nothing. I'm just suspicious. If something does come out of it you won't be in for a shock. You'll be ready. That's why I'm telling you.

JIMMY Now that I come to think of it you could be right. You remember that morning she took up his breakfast.

SAMMY I wouldn't mind that.

JIMMY Then there was his socks. She volunteered to darn them. She volunteered.

SAMMY That don't mean anything.

JIMMY Always asking him what he'd like for his tea.

SAMMY That don't mean anything either.

JIMMY Then two and two don't make four. It seems as if I'll have to have a talk with Mister Eddie.

SAMMY Now's your chance. That's them at the door.

JIMMY Yesterday I would have trusted him with my life.

SAMMY You want to be careful what you say.

JIMMY Leave it to me.

(*Enter Mrs. Swan followed by Eddie.*)

MRS. SWAN (*Taking off her coat.*) I thought you two would be in the pub.

SAMMY The pubs are deserted.

MRS. SWAN Sit down Eddie. I'll make a pot of tea. Anybody like sandwiches?

(*All refuse.*)

MRS. SWAN I won't be long.

(*Exit Mrs. Swan.*)

JIMMY Sit down Eddie.

(*Eddie sits.*)

JIMMY Have a beer.

(*Jimmy hands him a bottle. Sammy hands him a glass. Eddie pours.*)

JIMMY So what did you do to-night Eddie?

EDDIE We had a walk. We went right down by the river.

JIMMY Go far?

EDDIE We must have done three miles all told, that would be going and coming.

SAMMY You chaps will excuse me.

JIMMY Stay where you are.

SAMMY No, no I can't. I got bags to pack. Anyway I'm tired, my eyes are starting to close. Good night.

(*Exit Sammy in a hurry*).

EDDIE What's the matter with him?

JIMMY Don't know. You notice something?

EDDIE Not particularly just that he's always the last to go to bed.

JIMMY Never mind him for now. How did the walk go?

EDDIE Very nice. Saw a salmon leaping in the big pool near the Sally Grove. Must've been twenty pounds.

JIMMY Anything else?

EDDIE Saw a kingfisher. Wouldn't have known what it was but for your mother.

JIMMY A kingfisher eh? Anything else?

EDDIE Let me see now . . . Water was nice. Clear as crystal. Oh yes, we saw an otter swimming a good ways off. You know where the bend is? . . . well it was right there. Now that I come to think of it a flight of swans went by. By jove they make some noise, don't they? I don't recall much else.

JIMMY You sure?

EDDIE (*Now aware that something's afoot.*) That's as much as I recall offhand. We met some folk from the village, friends of your mother and there were some children tossing stones from the bridge. What's all the questions for anyway?

JIMMY You'll see. Just sit tight and you'll see.

53

JIMMY You've been out with my mother several times now.

EDDIE Yes I have.

JIMMY This is a very serious matter. Once or twice might not be too bad but several times.

EDDIE It's been above board.

JIMMY So you say. What's between you two?

EDDIE Actually I meant to speak to you about that this very night.

JIMMY You did, did you?

EDDIE Yes, I did but I think your mother would like to be here. I'll call her in.

(He goes to exit and calls.)

EDDIE Mary . . . Would you step in a moment please.

JIMMY So it's Mary now is it?

EDDIE It's been Mary right from the beginning.

JIMMY And I suppose she calls you Eddie.

EDDIE Yes, she does.

JIMMY This is downright slinky.

EDDIE Calling each other by our christian names. What's slinky about that?

JIMMY Well if you want to know I think it's too damn familiar. But that's not all. A lot's been happening behind my back and I don't think I like it. In fact I think it's time a stop was put to it.

(Enter Mary Swan.)

MARY *(To Eddie.)* You called?

EDDIE I thought it better.

MARY Have you told him?

EDDIE Not yet.

(Jimmy suddenly jumps to his feet.)

JIMMY Told me what? What in hell's blazes is going on here. *(Looks from one to the other.)* For God's sake what is it? This is a nice carry-out. I don't know what's happening under my own roof.

MARY You'd better tell him.

EDDIE Yes. I'd better.

54

JIMMY By God you'd better because I have reached a point where I can't take any more.

EDDIE I won't be going back to England with you chaps in the morning. I'll be staying on here.

JIMMY You can't stay on here.

EDDIE Your mother and I intend to get married very soon.

JIMMY Married! But you can't get married.

EDDIE Why not?

JIMMY Because she's my mother, that's why not.

EDDIE What has that got to do with it?

JIMMY You'd be my father. It's ridiculous.

MARY It's got nothing to do with you really but we thought it would be proper to tell you.

JIMMY What do you mean it's got nothing to do with me? You're my mother aren't you? I never heard anything so outlandish in my life. You're years older than he is. You'll be the laughing stock of the village.

EDDIE See here. . . .

MARY You look after the tea Eddie and don't come 'till I call.

EDDIE Very well . . . if that's what you want.

(*Exit Eddie.*)

MARY Maybe I will be the laughing stock of the village but only for a while. Then the people will get used to it the way they get used to everything. I used to be the pity of the village. People used to feel sorry for me when a year and then two years passed and you didn't show up but it was only a matter of time 'till they got used to it. They got used to it before I did.

JIMMY So we're back to that again.

MARY I couldn't bear the pity on their faces and I would stay indoors for days. They meant well. They wanted to help. I used to pray they wouldn't notice.

It was so embarrassing. Then one of the neighbour's children would come home for the summer holidays and another might come at Easter or Whit. At Christmas the crowds would come. Those first Christmases I used to hide my head. I stayed in bed all of one

Christmas day. I didn't eat anything. I didn't need it. I was waiting for Christmas to go away so's I could get up and get out.

JIMMY Belt up mother, will you please.

MARY No Jimmy. You listen. There were boys and girls in the village who had no reason to come back. They never saw anything here. It was different with you. I never gave you cause not to come. I did all in my power to raise you properly.

JIMMY I meant to come. Not coming is a habit you get into. You must believe that. You mean to come. Then a year passes and another and it's an extra bad habit. Don't get married again. He'll bore you stiff anyway. All he talks about is woods and fields and inland places with water. He never lets up on the water.

MARY You'll be always welcome to come home for a holiday Jimmy.

JIMMY You're determined then.

MARY Yes, I'm determined.

JIMMY You know what this means.

MARY Tell me.

JIMMY It means I can never come home again.

MARY What you're saying is if I get married you'll never come home again. Don't you want me to be happy. Getting married means I won't be lonely anymore.

JIMMY You get married to him and you'll never see me again.

MARY It was nine years last time Jimmy. If it's as long this time it won't make any difference.

JIMMY Why in God's name did I ever bring his with me?

MARY It's the other way round Jimmy. Why in God's name did he ever bring you?

CURTAIN.

THE PURE OF HEART

A play in one act

CHARACTERS IN ORDER OF APPEARANCE:

MURT O'BRIEN

BARTHOLOMEW

ALAPHONSUS FONCE

Action takes place at a country crossroads. The adjacent hedges are in full bloom. The time is June. It is approaching dawn. From nearby comes the sound of running water. Here and there crickets sing and in the far distance a dog barks. A man who has been sitting still on a milestone rises and walks upstage where he peers to left and right of him. He shakes his head in sorrow and disappointment. He looks at his watch, purses his lips and decides to wait yet awhile. Hands behind his back he paces back and forth. As his back is turned a head appears from behind a hedge and surveys him. It is the head of a middleaged man, grey-haired, weatherbeaten and with every line that the years could give. The man who paces the stage is Murt O'Brien. Again he looks at his watch and shakes his head. Again he looks left and right. As he turns his head the other ducks his. The other is Bartholomew Lane. Suddenly Murt O'Brien senses that there is something amiss. He still paces back and forth and each time his back is turned the head of Bartholomew Lane appears to watch his movements. Murt is most sensitive now and almost certain that he is being watched. He wheels about unexpectedly and catches the other fair and square.

MURT **Stand where you are.**

57

BARTH Yes sir, certainly sir.

MURT And don't call me sir. I have no more than you.

BARTH Of course you haven't.

MURT Come out here where I can get a proper look at you.

BARTH Right away sir. I was just about to come out anyway.

(*He clambers through hedge and stands with his hat in his hand respectfully.*)

MURT What are you—that hides behind a hedge peeping at honest men?

BARTH My name is Bartholomew Lane. I wasn't peeping.

MURT It was mighty like it. Are you a water bailiff?

BARTH No.

MURT A poacher?

BARTH No.

MURT You're putting down pishogues that's what you're at. June is a great month for the evil eye.

BARTH God forbid I'd ever do such a thing. My main purpose is to cross this road and go on about my business.

MURT There's no one stopping you.

BARTH That's good to hear. I'll be on my way then. I have seven cows to milk and calves to feed. Every cock in the countryside will be crowing shortly. Good luck to you.

MURT Wait a minute. You didn't tell me what your business was, why you hid behind the hedge like a criminal, why you had to seek my permission to cross the road. What are you anyway?

BARTH I might ask the same of you.

MURT Oh no. I have nothing to hide. My business is open and above board. I came here to meet a girl. You didn't by any chance meet her, a blue eyed little thing with red hair?

BARTH I saw nothing.

MURT You saw me. Now what are you?

BARTH I'm a red-blooded man that's what I am.

MURT What's that supposed to mean?

BARTH I'm after leaving a woman. That's what it means.

MURT Men left women before this and they didn't hide behind hedges.

BARTH Granted but you see this woman happens to have a husband.

MURT A mighty amount of women have husbands.

BARTH This particular husband is off serving in the army.

MURT You're an adulterer then.

BARTH If that means to console a grass widow I'm it.

MURT That's why you hide.

BARTH That's why. I have no choice but to duck and dodge. I dare not expose myself. If I couldn't cross the road at this point I'd have to strip and cross the river. In water as it is I'd be lucky to keep a dry chin.

MURT You're old enough now to have a wife of your own.

BARTH And wise enough to know better. Another man's wife costs nothing, and tell me who'll miss a slice off a cut loaf. Eh?

MURT Why don't you marry? You're still not too old.

BARTH What I want I can't get and what I can get I don't want. You need big money and transport for them with looks. I have no money and no motor car. I make do with what I can get. I'll tell you this though my friend, I have three things that most men haven't.

MURT What would they be?

BARTH I have an ear for music, an eye for women and a tooth for whiskey.

MURT There's many would consider those to be vices.

BARTH Those who haven't got them would. You never told me what you were doing here pacing the road and it facing daybreak.

MURT You never asked me.

BARTH I'm asking you now.

MURT I was to meet a girl here.

BARTH And she never showed up?

MURT That would seem to be the case.

BARTH Are you waiting long?

MURT I'm here since ten.

BARTH 'Tis now four o'clock in the morning.

MURT Well I was thinking that when she didn't come herself she might send an account.

BARTH God preserve your innocence!

MURT You mean you never waited that long for a woman?

BARTH Oh I did indeed. I often waited for a month 'till her husband would be gone.

MURT That's different . . . Here . . . sit down and we'll have a jaw.

(*They seat themselves.*)

MURT Are you from the neighbourhood?

BARTH A mile down the river. You can see my place from the main road. There's a green hayshed and a clump of spruce to the lee of the house.

MURT And the grass widow?

BARTH She's handy and she's no burden. She's accommodating which is more than can be said of the rest of the women round here.

MURT Is she in love with you?

BARTH Naw.

MURT Are you in love with her?

BARTH Not now. I was earlier.

MURT Doesn't your conscience bother you?

BARTH Why should it?

MURT You're committing adultry.

BARTH That word again.

MURT I imagine my conscience would worry me.

BARTH A conscience my friend is no match for the touch of flesh. Tell me about this girl you were to meet.

MURT You might know her. Small, blue-eyed with reddish hair.

BARTH Go on.

MURT She has freckles.

BARTH Where?

MURT On her face of course. Where do you think?

BARTH Oh faith you'll find many a freckle going with the female belly.

MURT She'd be no more than twenty. A lively piece. I

was to pick her up at this cross at ten o'clock. This is the River Crossroads isn't it?

BARTH Dead right it is. Were you here on time?

MURT I was here twenty minutes before time just in case. My car is parked up the road there under the whitethorn. I was to take her to the dance in town.

BARTH Where did you meet her first?

MURT At a dance a week ago. I tried her for a date but she had her purse and compact given to another fellow so I asked if we might meet another night.

BARTH And she said alright, that she'd meet you here at the cross at ten o'clock, Friday the twenty first of June?

MURT Exactly.

BARTH You're only one of a thousand victims my friend. I know the dame in question. She's the only daughter to Bill Guck the farmer. She's Bridgie Guck, red-haired, hearty and handsome and as tidy a bit of a girl as ever kept a man waiting all night at a crossroads.

MURT 'Tis a game with her then is it?

BARTH I'm afraid so my friend. She does it all the time. From now 'till the end of September 'twill be a bad night indeed she won't have someone here waiting for her.

MURT 'Tis a mean sort of trick.

BARTH My friend since Moses came down from the mountain and before, the wisest of men have fallen for the same trick and they'll keep on falling for it 'till Gabriel tootles his bugle and calls an end to the game.

MURT You know it all don't you?

BARTH No I don't my friend. I fell for it too many a time down the years but I learned that a well-anchored grass widow is a safer prospect for the likes of me. A man that learns that much has learned more than any scholar. I used to aim high one time too like you. Then as time passed I found my true range. I'm seldom off target now. I can't afford to be. My ammunition is likely to run out without warning.

MURT This woman of yours. What's she like?

61

BARTH Past her prime a bit. Alright though. She'll make no promises she can't keep. I'm sure she does have other callers but that's her business, not mine. What matters is that she does be there when I need her.

MURT I understand. Might I ask if you're happy?

BARTH I don't know. I have no complaints about the world, not anymore. I have my health. I have a roof over my head, a good fire and a good bed when I want them.

MURT A woman too . . . when you want her.

BARTH That's not too often now . . . but it's often enough. I suppose you could say I'm happy. Happy enough.

MURT What about the grace of God?

BARTH Now why did you have to go and spoil everything with a question like that?

MURT Sorry. I shouldn't have asked. Forget it.

BARTH No. I know God so it could be said I have God and if I have God I have his grace. I make my God to suit me. No one will adopt a God that doesn't suit them.

MURT Is that honest?

BARTH Maybe not but we can't be too hard on ourselves. The world is hard enough without God being hard as well. Every man must mould his God to suit himself. My God is an easy-going sort of fellow. Hush . . . there are footsteps on the road. Hush . . . they're coming this way.

MURT I can hear.

BARTH 'Tis not the dainty step of Bridgie Guck.

MURT 'Tis a heavy tread sure enough.

(*Barth peers in the direction of the steps.*)

MURT Do you know who it is?

BARTH No, only that it's a man.

MURT 'Tis a strange hour for a man to be abroad.

BARTH We're abroad. Now ask yourself why we're abroad. The answer you'll get is women. Whoever this man is you may be sure that his business concerns the opposite sex.

(*Enter a tramp. He wears a long black overcoat, a hat, sandals without socks and upon his back a rucksack. He is Alaphonsus Fonce. He also carries a stout stick.*)

ALAPHONSUS Good-night gentlemen.

BOTH Good-night.

ALAPHONSUS Is that a river I hear chortling close by?

MURT Yes. There's a river just inside the hedge.

ALAPHONSUS How fortunate. My name gentlemen is Alaphonsus Fonce. I'm a wandering bard.

MURT This is Bartholomew Lane and I am Murt O'Brien.

ALAPHONSUS How deep is this river?

BARTH It's deep enough in places.

ALAPHONSUS Then I won't venture far from the bank. (*He proceeds to undress.*) I bathe but once a year and then I bathe only in June. Less risk of catching a chill and the water is never cold. June is a mighty month men. If men and women don't make the most of June the bloom will fade from the world. (*As he undresses it can be seen that he wears no shortcoat. Under the overcoat which he discards he wears a necktie. He also wears a trousers. Underneath he wears a large pair of ladies knickers which extend from his navel to his knees.*)

MURT I see you wear no vest.

ALAPHONSUS I'll wait 'till I see the wild geese before I pull a vest over my head. (*Alaphonsus crouches over his rucksack and goes through it's contents.*) There's a small knob of soap here someplace. Ah here it is. (*He rises. He pats his ample paunch, takes a deep breath and flexes his shoulders.*) I've half a mind to gallop through the countryside in my pelt. June always does this to me. I long to be free of my garments, to shed the burden of my apparel and be away like a stag through the blooming fields.

BARTH Throw off your drawers and gallop away. We'll keep an eye on your things.

ALAPHONSUS It's not so easy.

63

BARTH Who's to stop you?

ALAPHONSUS My fellows. I tried it before, five years ago at a place called the Curate's Cross. There was a stream by the road and after I bathed I gave a great screech, like a stallion, and tore across the fields to dry myself. I must have woke the countryside. They came at me with pikes and spades and shovels. One bucko, if you don't mind, tried to dismember me on the spot we all cherish. I was lucky to escape. No more naked gallops for me. Let horses and asses do that. No one minds them.

MURT You're a man for Summer then?

ALAPHONSUS And for Spring and for Autumn but for Winter no.

MURT What do you do in Winter?

ALAPHONSUS I hibernate in one of the County Homes until I see the daffodils. Then hang the lot of 'em, it's the open road for me.

MURT It's a life I could never take to.

ALAPHONSUS Each man must go his own road. I'd look nice wouldn't I, tied down like the pair of you. Where's the gap to the river?

BARTH (*Points.*) Through there. Take care.

ALAPHONSUS (*Looks upward and around appreciatively.*) Oh June, June! You crazy bitch. You've gone to my head once more!

(*Exit Alaphonsus.*)

MURT What do you make of him?

BARTH Like all of his kind, respects nothing. By his own admission he runs round naked.

MURT A dreadful thing. Would you do it?

BARTH The seldom time I'm naked I don't run. Listen to me now my friend, we'll have the dawn of day breathing down our necks in less than an hour. You're too good a cut of a man to be wasting your time mooning over a woman that made a fool of you. 'Tis shaping for a fine day and as your man said there's a bloom in the world. June is for love my friend, not for moping. A night like this calls for the act of love. Dreams are for fools when summer is at it's height. We'll have the winter long if we want to dream. Did you ever stop to think that it might be the last summer either of us will see?

MURT What are you driving at?

BARTH Over yonder at the base of that hill there's a white-washed cottage roofed with sheets of corrugated iron. You can't miss it. In that cottage there's a fine ball of a woman thrown down on her back in a roomy bed. Her eyes are open wide and she's looking up at the ceiling, listening to the sounds of June. She can't sleep. It's not a night for sleep and anyway there's a hunger in this woman, a fierce and unholy hunger that only comes in the height of summer. This is a great chance for you. This is what is known as a golden opportunity. She's there and she's waiting. She's wishing and she's longing.

(*From inside the hedge comes a great roar, followed by a succession of shorter roars, grunts and exclamations of all kinds.*)

MURT He's after taking the plunge.

BARTH More luck to him. Are you paying attention to what I'm saying?

MURT You said this woman was wishing and longing.

BARTH Exactly.

MURT But with you only after leaving her how could she have such a longing?

BARTH I didn't leave a dint on her man. What am I but a rusty blade. 'Tis you that has the edge. You're young and fresh.

MURT I'd have to think hard before I'd do that. Maybe some other time.

BARTH It won't be the same some other time. You don't know women. This is her time. Go on away with you while the going is good. The blossom of June itself is on this woman tonight. It won't keep forever. Blossoms fade and die. I can almost hear her sighing from here.

(*Alaphonsus bursts through the hedge gasping and grunting. He trots round puffing and panting. He is covered with water drops. Suddenly he lies on his back.*)

BARTH Well?

MURT I don't know.

BARTH You're a fool man if you don't go.

MURT 'Twould be wrong.

BARTH 'Twould be wrong not to go.

MURT How do I know she'll have me?

BARTH You have my word. She'll turn no respectable man from her door at this time.

MURT I've never in my life seen her.

BARTH You say I sent you. You say I was sent by Bartholomew Lane.

MURT Suppose her husband turns up?

BARTH Her husband is a hundred miles away snoring off an overdose of beer. He don't know she's alive not to mind knowing of her needs and wants. I'll crave you no more.

(*Alaphonsus sits up, keenly interested.*)

BARTH Why should I? I'm putting a great favour your way and you're half-hearted.

MURT Suppose the children wake?

BARTH There are no children.

MURT What about the neighbours?

BARTH There's no house within two miles of her.

MURT Has she a dog?

BARTH She has.

MURT Suppose he attacks?

BARTH Great God you're an awful man for supposing. A man that supposes like you will never be a day's good to anyone. I'll tell you no more but this last time. When you come within hailing distance of the cottage let you whistle three times like this. (*Barth emits three rounds of similar whistles.*) The whistling will alert her and the dog will wag his tail thinking 'tis me. In case he don't wag his tail you call him by his name which is Bonzo. You say quietly; down Bonzo, down boy.

Pat him on the forehead and if he don't respond kick his behind. That'll settle him. Tap gently then on the window on the right hand side and when she asks who's out say like I told you: 'I was sent by Bartholomew Lane.' You'll gain admission no bother. My advice to you is make the most of it because soon 'twill be cockcrow and that will be another day.

MURT No I couldn't.

BARTH Why not?

MURT I'd be an adulterer.

BARTH I can see you're determined to let that word get the better of you.

MURT Anyway, I might be seen.

(*Aalphonsus rises.*)

ALAPHONSUS What is this woman's name?

BARTH Now . . . now, it's nothing to do with you.

ALAPHONSUS Are you her owner then?

BARTH Of course not.

ALAPHONSUS Then what's her name?

BARTH Her name is Kitty.

ALAPHONSUS Kitty is it? I like it. Kitty, Kitty, Kitty. Here Kitty.

(*Alaphonsus sings*):
Kitty my love will you marry me
Kitty my love will you go
Kitty my love will you marry me
Either say yes or say no.

BARTH You'd want to stay in your place my friend.

ALAPHONSUS You say the dog's name is Bonzo. (*Roars with authority.*) Down Bonzo. Down sir. Down you common cur. And the woman's name is Kitty.

BARTH She'll have nothing to do with your likes. She bars the door against your kind.

ALAPHONSUS What is my kind?

BARTH Anyone can see you're a tramp.

ALAPHONSUS (*To Murt.*) Is that what I am? A tramp?

MURT So it would seem.

ALAPHONSUS But how will fair Kitty know I'm a tramp?

MURT Anyone could tell that.

ALAPHONSUS But how?

MURT Your get-up.

ALAPHONSUS You mean my clothes?

MURT Yes.

ALAPHONSUS But not by my demeanour?

MURT Your what?

ALAPHONSUS My demeanour, my manner, my disposition
Look at me. How can you tell what I am? Here I
stand clad in bright water drops and one outsize pair
of shopsoiled, ladies knickers. There is no man and
there is no woman on the face of this earth who can
say what I am as I present myself now. I could be the
county surgeon or the county engineer. I could be the
inspector of schools or I could be the inspector of
taxes. If I said I was a district court judge who would
doubt me? My skin glistens with beads of river water.
My body is washed clean. Am I not worthy of this
country Kitty, this poor soul who has known only
oafs and louts and a drunkard of a husband?

BARTH You better not.

ALAPHONSUS This woman belongs to this time known as
June and not to you. But what shall I be? I think I'll
be a professor, that's it, a professor. I'll be a professor
of small vowels and uncommon consonants. And my
story. Yes . . . of course. I was camping by the river-
side when I was awakened by intruders. I rose, dressed
only as you see me now and gave chase. Unhappily, I
fell into the river. I stumbled upon your cottage by
accident. My name is Professor Alaphonsus Fonce.
Sorry for the intrusion.

MURT You wouldn't dare.

ALAPHONSUS It's twelve months since I had my arms
round a woman.

BARTH You can't. I won't allow it.

ALAPHONSUS Won't allow it? Don't make me laugh. Over
yonder is a languishing dame stretched on the flat of
her back and here am I hungering these twelve miser-

68

able months for a woman. (*Stretches out his arms to their extremities.*) Don't stand in the way of nature you fool! (*Looks upwards and round.*) Oh June, you flaming, fleeting jade. You crazy bitch. You perfumed budding beauty. (*To Bartholomew Lane.*) Out of my way. Times like these will never come again.

BARTH You're not going.

MURT That's right. Get your clothes on and move along. We don't want your kind interfering with our women-folk. (*Finds a fairly large stone unseen by Alaphonsus and awaits his chance.*)

ALAPHONSUS Your womenfolk indeed. That's a good one. We'll let her decide whose woman she is. Now clear the way, I've waited long enough.

BARTH You'll suffer damage if you don't do as you're told.

ALAPHONSUS What is this?

BARTH We don't know you.

ALAPHONSUS You see me don't you? I'm not deformed. I'm not lice-ridden. I've had a fine wash. My paunch is without a wrinkle. I'm of sound mind. I have nothing the matter with me.

BARTH Who knows what you have? Now move along smart and tangle with your own kind. You'll find plenty doxies in the town.

ALAPHONSUS You're not stopping me. Nothing can stop me. My love is on the broad of her back. I must attend to her. I'm away . . .

MURT You're away alright. (*Hits him on back of head with stone. Alaphonsus falls to the ground with a moan.*)

BARTH That was a quare flake you hit him.

MURT 'Twas that or have a woman raped.

BARTH Raped?

MURT Yes. Raped. You heard him didn't you?
(*They both survey the fallen Alphonsus.*)

BARTH (*Bending to listen.*) There's no noise coming from him, no noise at all. I don't like the look of him.

MURT Let's take him to the river.

BARTH Yes. The very thing. 'Twill make no difference once we throw him in.

(*Murt drags him to the gap and aided by Barth gets him through. Exit Murt and Alaphonsus. Barth gathers the effects of Alaphonsus and flings them over the hedge. (He looks around to make sure that there is nothing left behind. He looks all round and calls.*)

BARTH Is it done?

MURT (*From inside hedge.*) Done.

BARTH Are you sure his head is under?

MURT It's under.

BARTH Is there bubbles?

MURT There's no vubbles.

BARTH What are you waiting for then?

(*Enter Murt through gap.*)

MURT Do you think it will be alright?

BARTH Of course it will. He has no roots. No one cares. When they see the way he's dressed they'll think he was off his rocker or drunk to begin with. They'll think he fell on the stones and struck the back of his head. They wouldn't believe us even if we admitted it.

MURT Let's get out of here. It's almost daybreak.

BARTH Aren't you going to call on the woman?

MURT No.

BARTH But you killed for her.

MURT Did I?

BARTH Yes you did. Rather than see her soiled by a tramp you killed him. Go and see her. You'll need her now. Believe me.

MURT No. I can't. 'Twould be a mortal sin. 'Twould stay in my conscience. I'm going to my home and if you've any sense you'll go to yours. (*He moves towards exit.*) If I can't have a woman the honest way I won't have her at all. I won't be an adulterer.

(*Exit Murt.*

Barth stands, deep in thought. In the distance a dog barks and a cock crows three times.)

70   CURTAIN.

MORE PLAYS BY JOHN B. KEANE

THE FIELD

The Field is a play about the social and moral effects of land greed. 'A fine play of living dialogue, even in its vulgarity and profanity, with characters that come from the author's real understanding of the people, the problems, and evils of our rural community.' *Standard.*

85342 254 0   50p

THE MAN FROM CLARE

Personal tragedy of an ageing athlete who finds he no longer has the physical strength to maintain his position as captain of the team, and his reputation as the best footballer in Clare.

85342 092 0   77 pp.   35p

THE YEAR OF THE HIKER

The 'Hiker' is the much hated father who deserted his wife and family twelve years previously and whose return is awaited with fear. This play portrays with tears and laughter the fears and happiness of the Lacey family.

85342 090 4   94 pp.   35p

BIG MAGGIE

The theme of this play is the domination of an Irish family by a hard and tyrannical mother, and it brings out all the humour and pathos of Irish rural life.

85342 093 9   94 pp. (Hardcover)   £1.25

MOLL

'When a presbytery gets a new housekeeper it becomes like a country that gets a change of government, or like a family that gets a new stepmother', says Fr. Brest when Canon Pratt is about to hire their new housekeeper, Miss Mollie Kettle, alias 'Moll'. These are the first forebodings of the calamity that is about to befall them. So 'Moll' is hired, establishes her regime, the Canon and parish begin to prosper, the curates suffer . . . She gets a choir going, the church is repaired, a new school is built—yet the curates groan under their share in the household chores.

Hilariously funny, *Moll*, will entertain and amuse everybody.

85342 281 8   80 pp.   40p

THE CHANGE IN MAME FADDEN

Remembering such plays as *The Field* and *Big Maggie,* one thinks at once of the people in them: earthy, self-willed, gifted with a salty wit of their own. Mame Fadden in this play is equally memorable: maddeningly human but of tragic dimensions. We watch her inevitable progress towards her ultimate crisis; this is a woman pushed to the limit. Her story is the more poignant for being enacted against a background of suburban comfort, but Mame and her problems are universal. For twenty years she has sacrificed everything for her husband and her sons. Now she faces the physical and mental upheaval of the change of life. She asks—begs—for sympathy and love. Her family can respond only with gestures as obtuse as they are well-meaning. They simply do not understand. That is Mame's tragedy.

85342 332 6   104 pp.   65p